A Child's Look at the Twenty-third Psalm

A Child's Look at the Twenty-third Psalm

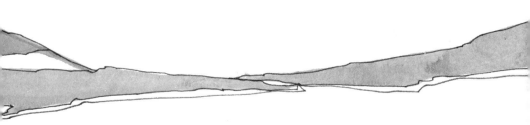

W. PHILLIP KELLER

Illustrated by Lauren Jarrett

A DOUBLEDAY-GALILEE BOOK

Doubleday & Company, Inc., Garden City, New York   1985

BY THE SAME AUTHOR:

Sea Edge
Joshua — Man of Fearless Faith
A Layman Looks at the Love of God
Lessons from a Sheep Dog
Wonder O'the Wind
Salt for Society
A Layman Looks at the Lamb of God
On Wilderness Trails
Elijah — Prophet of Power
Walking with God
Still Waters
Expendable
Taming Tension
Ocean Glory

Mountain Splendor
Mighty Man of Valor — Gideon
A Gardener Looks at the Fruit
of the Spirit
A Shepherd Looks at the Good Shepherd
and His Sheep
Rabboni — Which is to Say, Master
A Layman Looks at the Lord's Prayer
A Shepherd Looks at Psalm 23
Bold Under God —
A Fond Look at a Frontier Preacher
As a Tree Grows
Splendor from the Sea

Library of Congress Cataloging in Publication Data
Keller, W. Phillip (Weldon Phillip), 1920-
A child's look at the Twenty-third Psalm.
"A Doubleday-Galilee book."
Summary: Explores the meaning of the twenty-third psalm
in which Christ's love for his followers is likened to
that of a shepherd for his flock.
1. Bible. O.T. Psalms XXIII — Criticism, interpretation,
etc. — Juvenile literature. [1. Bible. O.T. Psalms XXIII]
I. Jarrett, Lauren, ill. II. Bible. O.T. Psalms XXIII.
III. Title.
BS1450 23rd.K4   1985   223'.206   84-13718
ISBN 0-385-15457-7 (pbk.)

ISBN: 0-385-15456-9
Library of Congress Catalog Card Number 80-976

First Edition

To My Grandchildren
and All Other Children
Who Open This Book

Author's Note

When I was first asked to write a children's book, the idea seemed incongruous. Never before had I even considered such a project. I had always written for adults. Beyond that, it seemed I was too far advanced in years and out-of-touch with children to tackle such a project.

On the other hand, if, in the twilight of my life, my Father in Heaven was opening a new field of service, who was I to refuse such an opportunity. New challenges have always appealed to my adventuresome spirit. So, with God's help, I decided to try. This little book is the result.

In it I have attempted to step back in time more than fifty years: to speak as a child speaks, to see as a child sees, to imagine as a child does, to communicate as a child does.

May our Father bless the book and enrich you, the reader, with it.

W. Phillip Keller
"Still Waters"
1980

Before We Begin

God is a real person. He is very kind. He is very strong. He is very wise. He is very fond of us. He knows all about us. He loves to show us what He is really like. This is wonderful. It helps us understand Him. It keeps us from having wrong ideas about Him.

The first way He shows Himself to us is in Jesus Christ. When Jesus lived here among us, He said, "He that has seen me has seen the Father" (John 14:9).

This same Jesus also said He was our Good Shepherd (John 10:11-16). A shepherd is a person who takes care of sheep. He usually owns the sheep. If he is a good shepherd, he gives all his time, care, and strength to them. He does this because he loves them and wants them to do well.

Long ago a man called David, who had been a shepherd, wrote a lovely poem about sheep. It is called Psalm 23. Thousands of people love this poem. It tells the story of a sheep's life in the care of a good shepherd. It is a word picture of our Lord Jesus Christ. The poem is written as though a sheep was speaking to its friends about the wonderful shepherd who owns it.

That is exactly the way I am talking to you, my friends, about Jesus Christ who is our Good Shepherd. It is an exciting story. It is full of good news about our Lord God.

The Twenty-third Psalm

The Lord is my shepherd; I shall not want.

He maketh me to lie down in green pastures: he leadeth me beside the still waters.

He restoreth my soul: he leadeth me in the paths of righteousness for his name's sake.

Yea, though I walk through the valley of the shadow of death, I will fear no evil: for thou art with me; thy rod and thy staff they comfort me.

Thou preparest a table before me in the presence of mine enemies: thou anointest my head with oil; my cup runneth over.

Surely goodness and mercy shall follow me all the days of my life: and I will dwell in the house of the Lord for ever.

The Lord — My Shepherd

"The Lord" is a favorite name for God. It is our way of saying that Jesus Christ is a wonderful person. He is greatest in all the world, in all the universe. He is the One who knows everything. Yet He is tender-hearted, patient, understanding.

Jesus Christ made the earth. It is exciting to think He first saw the oceans, rivers, lakes, and streams take their shape. He shaped mountains and hills. He formed valleys and plains. He stretched out the sky like a great curtain. He scattered stars in space. He set the sun, moon, and planet earth, where we live, in motion.

I love to think that He first saw grass, flowers, shrubs, and trees spring from the soil. They pleased Him. He made fish in the water, insects in the air, birds on wing, and animals on the plains and hills. He delighted in them all.

He also made people like you and me. Some white, others brown, yellow, red, and black. He loves us all. He calls us His children. He also calls us His sheep, because we often behave like sheep. We wander away from Him. We get into trouble.

Jesus is always ready to help us. He does not become moody or mean like some people. He understands us. He gives us His life, energy, and guidance to help us succeed. I just love this kind Shepherd. I hope you do too.

Who Does Own Me?

Not every shepherd is kind. Some who own sheep are cruel and careless. They do not love their flock. Their sheep suffer because they are lazy.

Sometimes their fields are bare and brown, with no green grass or sweet clover. The sheep have no shade from the burning sun. Even the water they drink is dirty. A bad shepherd does nothing to keep his sheep from getting sick. He does not care when ticks, flies, mosquitoes, or mites torment his flock. If stray dogs, wolves, cougars, or coyotes raid the sheep, he is not there to protect them.

Sheep with this sort of master have a miserable life. Sometimes they stand inside the fence of their bare fields and look with longing at the lush, green grass on the other side. How

they wish they could be free to follow the good shepherd on his lovely land.

Some of us are like that too. We never come into the good, generous care of God. We do not really know and follow Christ. We have never been set free from our old owner.

Who is that? It may be ourselves. We think we can be our own boss. We want to do our own thing, to go our own way. We are mastered by our selfish nature. It often keeps us in trouble. If we are wise, we will let Christ, the Good Shepherd, take over our lives. We do this by inviting Him into our hearts.

Coming Into the Good Shepherd's Care

There is always a very special affection between a shepherd who really loves sheep, and his flock. It is hard for many people to understand this. Let me explain clearly, so you will see the reasons.

First, his sheep have cost him a lot of money. They are the ones he chose with great care. Second, he takes them to his home ranch with joy. There he gives them the best of every-

thing. He does not spare his strength, his time, his skill, and his very life so that they thrive.

It is exactly the same with our Good Shepherd, Jesus Christ. He has bought us with the precious price of His very own life, which was poured out to pay for all our wrongs. Even though we have gone astray, He comes searching for us. He lays Himself out freely for our sakes. Like a shepherd seeking a lost lamb in the hills, He rescues us from our selfish ways.

He does this because He is *Love* itself. This sort of *Love* is the opposite of our selfishness. It is that strong, powerful *Love* that shares itself in helping and healing others, gladly, cheerfully.

That is the joyful news about Jesus, the Good Shepherd. In spite of our sins (wrongdoing)—in spite of our selfishness—in spite of how lost we may be, Jesus Christ comes to free us from our folly.

He enfolds us with His love. He comes with His strong, peaceful presence.

The Master's Mark

A good shepherd puts his own special earmark on his sheep. It is one or several cuts made in the right or left ear. Sometimes little notches may be put in both ears. The permanent mark shows up clearly when a sheep stands facing anyone. That way they can tell exactly who the owner is.

The marking is a painful little operation. The ear is laid on a small block of wood in the shepherd's strong hand. Then it is notched swiftly with a very sharp knife. From then on, everyone knows to whom that sheep or lamb belongs.

Sometimes the owner just paints or stamps a number or letter on the wool. But this only lasts a short time. When the wool grows out it is sheared off the sheep. So then it must be marked again and again.

When we belong to our Good Shepherd, Jesus Christ, He too puts a special mark on us. It is "The Master's Mark." By this mark anyone can tell that we belong to Him. Can you guess what it might be?

It is the mark of love which His own life leaves upon us. Like notching a lamb's ear it also comes with some suffering. We are those who are no longer selfish. We are not just interested in "me" and "mine" and "I". Rather, we care about others. We share with others. We take the time and trouble to help and cheer them just as Jesus does with us.

I Shall Not Want

This little sentence means much more than most of us understand. Picture in your mind a very pleased, happy, well-fed sheep, like the one facing this page. It is fit, frisky, and full of fun. It kicks up its heels as if it were exclaiming, "Because my owner, my manager, is such a good shepherd I lack nothing. I've got everything I want."

What a wonderful way to feel about life.

No complaining. No moaning. No grumbling.

Instead, this sheep and its companions are enjoying life. They are relaxed. They are satisfied. They are joyful because of their good shepherd's care.

The same thing can be true of us when we come into the care of our Good Shepherd. Anyone who will really let the Lord share life with him or her will find life can be exciting. Our days can be full of adventures with Jesus. This is because He is there to help us in every new experience.

Please don't misunderstand me. I am not saying everything will be fun and games. Like growing up, there will be hard lessons to learn. There will be tough new tasks to tackle. There will be strange, thrilling, steep trails to follow. All of them open up new adventures. We don't need to be afraid or the least bit uneasy. We can look ahead calmly, gladly, because the Good Shepherd is with us. In Him we trust.

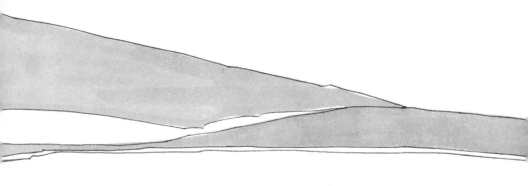

A Beautiful Ranch

If you want a real treat, take a drive through sheep country. Go down the narrow, winding, quiet roads that run through the hills and fields. You will find lovely farms where sheep graze peacefully in the grassy meadows. Sometimes flocks are so white they look like flower petals or snowflakes scattered on the green pastures.

The owner of a good sheep ranch is generally a kind, generous, big-hearted man. He will gladly show you his farm. He just loves it, and he loves his flock. A tender smile will crease his suntanned face, and a misty, loving look will fill his eyes as he leads you over his land. You can tell he gives all his strength and skill and money for his flock to make this farm beautiful. It is his life.

The spreading shady trees, the lush, rich fields, the handsome barns, the clear, clean, sparkling streams, the well-fed sheep, the peace—all tell of his tender care. No wonder the sheep are so satisfied. No wonder they enjoy living here. No wonder they don't wish to stray away from such a wonderful shepherd. They are so fond of his happy home.

It is that way too for those of us who learn to live and walk with our Good Shepherd. We come to feel right at home with Him. We are contented in His care. He makes life beautiful both for us and for Himself. His reputation is at stake in us. We enjoy walking with Him in safety.

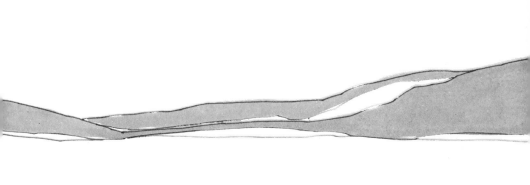

23

The Fence Crawler

It seems strange, yet it is often true, that even on the best of farms there can be a "fence crawler." That is the name given to a sheep that is not satisfied where it is. It always feels sure the grass on the other side of the fence is greener and sweeter than in its own home pastures.

For this reason a "fence crawler" is restless. If it is a mother sheep, called a ewe, she will carefully work her way along every fence or hedge, hoping to find a hole where she can push her way out. It may be a broken board, a loosened rail, a rusted wire, or even a gate someone forgot to close. Quickly she slips out through the opening. Her lambs or other sheep with her will follow her, forcing their way into the neighbor's fields.

This creates problems for everyone. The good shepherd wonders where his lost sheep have gone. He must drop everything to go and search for them. Often the sad thing is the sheep end up on poor pasture, or on a road, or even go astray to be stolen by strangers.

Some of us are like that. We are never satisfied with the way Christ cares for us. We are forever finding fault. We are

always looking for some new mischief, and we lead others to follow our example. We often get ourselves in trouble. And we cause our Good Shepherd heartache and grief.

He maketh me to lie down in green pastures:
he leadeth me beside the still waters.

Freedom from Fear

Sheep are easily frightened. Even a rabbit bursting out of the grass unexpectedly will panic a whole flock. The same thing happens if a stray dog, a wild animal, or even a strange person suddenly appears in the pasture.

Sheep are not big, strong, sturdy animals like cattle or horses. They do not have long claws or fierce teeth to fight off enemies. They are timid, almost helpless creatures. Their main defense is simply to jump up and dash away when danger comes.

Because of this they cannot relax or rest in the green pastures as long as they are afraid. They will be on their feet, ready to run. They are uneasy, they do not thrive or grow strong.

The surprising and wonderful thing is that when the shepherd is there, they feel safe. When he is near, their fears fade away. They settle down, and soon they are at rest.

We sometimes have fears. When something new or frightening happens to us we want to run or hide. We think the best defense is simply to get away.

Really, we don't have to live like that. Jesus Christ, our Good Shepherd, is always near. He tells us, *"I am with you always."*

How does one know? Turn to Him within your heart and spirit. Say quietly, "Thank you, Lord Jesus, for being here. Thank you for protecting me. I will not be afraid."

You will sense His presence with you.

Freedom from Quarreling

Remember I told you this story was like a sheep telling its friends all about its wonderful master? One thing that really pleased this sheep was that its shepherd was always nearby. It could lie down gently in the green pastures he had provided. It did not need to be afraid of strange animals or strange people that came on the ranch.

On the other hand, its peace can be disturbed by other sheep, even those from its own flock. You see, sheep and lambs quarrel, fight and butt each other. Often the stronger ones abuse the weaker. They butt and shove with their heads and shoulders. Sometimes the timid ewes and lambs have a hard time. They get little rest because of the bullies in the bunch.

But all of this suddenly changes as soon as their owner steps into sight. All their eyes turn toward him. This takes their attention off each other. The fighting ends. Soon all of them settle down quietly in the cool green grass.

That is a great lesson for us to learn. We don't have to fight and quarrel with our companions, friends, or family. It is pos-

sible to live in peace with other people. We must remind ourselves that God, our Good Shepherd, is with us. He is watch-
ing us. He is here. He does care about what is happening to
us. This makes all the difference in our behavior. We get our
attention off others onto Him. He gives peace.

Freedom from Flies

As warm spring weather comes to the countryside, so do the bugs. There are many insects that torment sheep.

Flies are especially bad. Warble and bot flies, as well as nasal flies, buzz around their heads. They light on their faces and noses. There they lay their tiny eggs. These hatch into horrible larvae—worms—that work their way into the sheep's head and body, driving them wild.

So to keep off the flies, the sheep toss their heads, flick their ears, stamp their feet, or stampede under trees and into bushes for shelter. When the shepherd sees this, he puts a spray or repellent on their heads and bodies. This keeps the insects away. Then the flock is free to feed quietly in the meadows. They can even lie down and rest gently.

It is much the same with us. There are all sorts of little, irritating things that come along to "bug" us. We get so upset and disturbed by petty little peeves or fiddly frustrations that seem to fly in our faces. Sometimes we are sure they will drive us wild.

You can never get away from tiny troubles in life. But you can count on the Good Shepherd to come close and put His helping, healing hands on you. Ask Him to give you the oil of His sweet Spirit to cope with life's frustrations. He will.

Growing Green Pastures

Most breeds of sheep do better in dry, semidesert country than where it is rainy and wet. This is because there are fewer insects and less disease in dry country.

So it means that many sheepmen have to work very hard to produce green pastures for their flocks. A good shepherd goes to great trouble to clear the rough, dry land of rocks, roots, and stumps. He must plow up and cultivate the soil, preparing a soft seed bed. Then he has to sow the grass and clover. In order for them to flourish, he must install an irrigation system to water the fields all through the hot summer weather.

All of this costs not only a lot of money, but also endless labor and skill and care. Yet he is happy to do it. He loves his sheep. He wants them well fed. He is thrilled and content at heart when he sees them so full they just want to lie down quietly to ruminate.

This is a beautiful picture of our Good Shepherd. The Lord Jesus Christ has made the earth a lovely place to live. It is rich

with grass, crops, cattle, and fruit to nourish us. It is also beautiful and inspiring for the good of our souls with its great forests, singing streams, lovely lakes, and surging seas. But our God also gives us green pastures of happy contentment in our spirits. We are at peace with Him, at peace with other people, at peace in ourselves.

How wonderful to belong to Christ!

Drinking the Dew

Not many people know sheep can easily quench their thirst with dew on the grass. If they are grazing in the meadows before dawn the pasturage is soaking wet. In fact, this is their favorite time of the whole day to feed. It is a very still and peaceful time. There is seldom any wind at break of day. The world lies quiet and silver bright under its covering of dew.

When the sun comes up, the air becomes warm. Breezes begin to blow. Dewdrops fall from the foliage. And soon the grass and clover are dry.

A good shepherd makes sure his sheep get out into the fields while they are drenched with the night dew. Even if it means he must get up very early to lead them into the silvery meadows, he is glad to do it for his flock.

He knows they will be both well fed and gently refreshed for the whole day.

It is very much like this with our own lives. Not many people know that the early morning is the best part of the whole day. Then the world is very still. There is hardly any noise, only an occasional bird song. In the coolness and quietness of the daybreak we can be so peaceful. We can think gently about our loving Lord.

This is a good time to speak to Him softly, to hear Him speak to us. It refreshes us, satisfies our hearts. It makes it a good day.

Water Wells

I would remind you again that most of the sheep in the world live in dry, hot country. Often there is not even dew on the grass. Sometimes there are no streams or springs or lakes where they graze. So water to refresh the flocks is hard to find.

The sheep rancher must go to tremendous labor and spend lots of money to dig deep wells for water. Sometimes the deep hole he digs is dry. There is no water. So he must try again and again.

When the diligent or hardworking shepherd finally strikes water, it is very precious. Even then he has to work hard to haul the water up to the surface. There he pours it into water

troughs to refresh his thirsty sheep. They come eagerly to drink under the blazing sun.

When Jesus Christ was among us, He invited people to come to Him and drink. He told them He could give them water to quench their thirst and satisfy their longing spirits.

Now we know that all the water in the world, whether in streams, lakes, rain or dew or even wells is a beautiful gift from God. It is His way of satisfying the thirst of our bodies.

In the same way, the thirst of our souls is satisfied best by Him. When we long for friendship, love, and peace the best place to go is to our Good Shepherd.

He gladly shares Himself with us. We are refreshed and satisfied by His precious friendship.

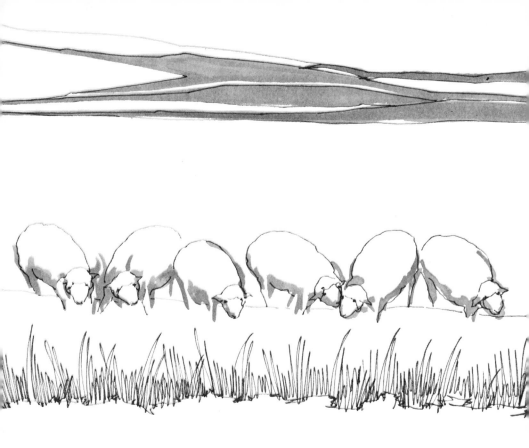

Singing Streams

If a flock of sheep live where there are streams, the shepherd loves to have them drink from the cool, clear waters. Many streams sing as they run happily from pool to pool. The water gurgles and laughs as it leaps from rock to rock, tumbling over its stony channel.

Here and there quiet pools of deep, clear, still water are to be found. That is where the sheep prefer to drink. There is nothing to disturb them. They are at peace.

Strange to say, some sheep, in their stupidity, will choose to drink from dirty pools and polluted ponds. Here the water is murky and dangerous. It is where the sheep often pick up disease. Because parasites—tiny, disease-producing forms of life— live in stale, stagnant water.

38

Some of us are like these foolish sheep. We seem to prefer to drink from the mudholes of our world. I do not mean just running the risk of drinking bad water, or even the dangers of toying with alcoholic drinks or drugs. But most important, I mean trying to satisfy ourselves with habits that can never fill our longing for the Lord.

You see, God made us for Himself. Only as we come to Him, whose life flows out happily like a singing stream, can we be fully refreshed, fully satisfied. In the still, quiet times with Him we can drink deeply of His wonderful friendship. We can be refreshed by His kindness to us.

A Cast Sheep

You may wonder what happened to this sheep. It has rolled onto its back and can't get up. It is cast. A bit like a little baby that is helpless.

For a shepherd this can be very serious, because it often happens to his biggest, fattest, and best ewes. For the ewe it can be very dangerous. She may even die if the shepherd does not come quickly to set her on her feet.

A sheep can be cast this way because of too much fat or too much heavy wool or just by accident. It rolls over too far while resting in a little hollow in the ground.

Wild birds like buzzards or wild animals like coyotes keep a careful lookout for helpless sheep they can attack. The sad thing is, it often happens when least expected.

Isn't our own life just like that? Sometimes it seems that when everything is going well, we are having fun and feeling

fine, suddenly we can get into trouble. One moment we are merry, the next moment we are in a mess.

Like this poor sheep, we can struggle and kick and try every trick to get out of our trouble. But, it seems, the harder we try the worse it becomes.

What we need is the help of our Good Shepherd to set us right again. He is the One who can come and lift us up. He will, because He loves us deeply.

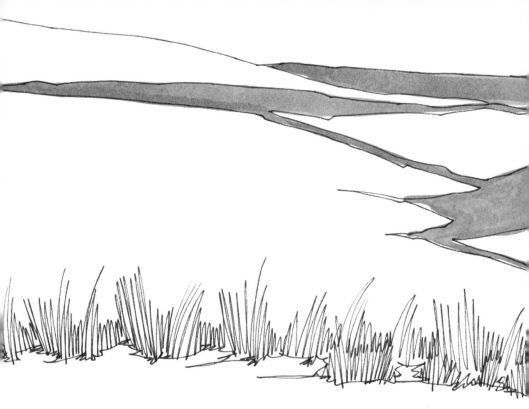

The Shepherd Saves His Sheep

A good shepherd counts his flock every day. Then he can tell if any are missing. If there is one lost, he will scan or look at the sky to see if buzzards are soaring over the range. It is often a sign that a sheep is cast on its back.

With racing heart he sets out to find his ewe. It is important to hurry. If the sun is hot the poor sheep may die in just a few hours. Or if wild animals are around they can easily kill it.

So the shepherd searches frantically. When he sees the sheep he runs to her. Gently he turns her over. He lifts her up in his strong arms. He sets her on her feet. For a few minutes he holds her upright between his own legs, rubbing the limbs to restore the blood supply.

Then, fully recovered, she is sent off, running happily to join the flock again.

This is a beautiful picture of what Jesus Christ is like. So

many people think that when they get into trouble God gets angry with them. No. He is not like that. Our Good Shepherd loves us so much, cares so deeply, He comes racing to rescue us.

He is the kind, gentle, strong Shepherd who picks us up. He holds us close. He speaks to us tenderly. He reassures us that He cares deeply what happens to us. He sets us on our way again, happy and glad to be rescued.

Shearing Sheep

Remember I said it is the biggest, fattest sheep that become cast. To stop this the owner shears the sheep. To shear means to clip off the wool. This is done in the hot weather so the sheep will not catch cold when its warm fleece is taken off. This is hard, dirty, smelly work. You see, the fleece of a sheep gets matted with mud, burrs, bugs, and manure.

All of these come off at shearing time. The sheep look much thinner. But that is a kindness because it cleans them up ready to go onto summer range. A good shepherd is willing to do this miserable job for the welfare of his flock.

There is a great lesson we can learn from this. It is easy for us to get sassy and proud. We think we are so strong or smart or sure of ourselves. It is just then that suddenly our pride puts us on our backs. Pride comes before a fall.

Sometimes our Master shows us up for what we are. His sharp, shearing words are:

"The last shall be first and the first shall be last."

This hurts, but it helps.

Sheep Following Sheep

Sheep have the habit of playing follow the leader. They just tag along behind one another without thinking where they are going. They walk along the same little twisted trails, graze on the same old dry, bare spots, drink from the same dirty pools, simply because the rest of the flock do it.

This is called the "mob instinct." It simply means that what one does, all the others do.

This habit in sheep does a lot of damage. It ruins beautiful ranches. It cuts gullies in the ground. It causes damage to the grass. Only an expert shepherd who manages his flock with great care can prevent or stop sheep from damaging his land.

People are a lot like sheep in this same habit. What one per-

son does, others do. Where one leader goes, others follow. Often we hear people say, "But everybody does it, so it must be all right."

This is not true. Some things that many people do, like cheating, lying, stealing, saying cruel things, may seem smart. But they are very evil and damaging. They hurt other people. They are selfish and foolish. Just because our friends go that way doesn't make it right.

Instead, Jesus Christ, our kind Shepherd, comes and offers to lead us in proper paths of helpful lives. He invites us to follow Him instead of the crowd. He can help us learn habits that are useful, kind, and loving.

Sheep Following the Shepherd

Happily, in the same way that sheep will follow one another, they will also follow a good shepherd. If they know him well and are fond of him, they go where he goes.

Because he wants them to flourish, he sees to it that his sheep are always on the move. He does not let them wear away the same winding trails. He does not allow them to overgraze and ruin the grass. He will keep them from muddy pools and polluted ponds.

The secret to his success with his sheep is to move them from one rich pasture to another. And the sheep learn to love this change. Every time he takes them into a fresh field they kick up their heels in frisky joy.

That is exactly how it can be if we follow our Good Shepherd. God wants us to be well, strong, joyful, useful people. He loves to lead us into new adventures and rich experiences of joy.

If you begin to do what He says, to go where He asks you, it will surprise you how wonderful the path of your life can be. The person who will go out of his own little selfish way to love and help others, who will share his time and fun and toys, will find life full of excitement. You will have days of great joy and pleasure that make you feel so good you will want to kick up your heels.

Trust Christ to guide you happily.

A Wayward Sheep

Once in a while there is a sheep that will not follow the shepherd. It would rather go its own way. It chooses to do its own thing. Maybe it feels it knows better than its owner where the best feed can be found.

Notice it is heading toward the trees in the forest. It thinks it is safe all on its own. It is so taken up with its own grazing it pays no attention to where its master the shepherd is going.

This wayward sheep is bound to get into trouble. Soon it may be lost in the woods. Or it will get so far separated from the shepherd he cannot find it easily. Or it may soon fall prey to a predator like a cougar or a coyote.

The sad thing is it really does not know it is in great danger all on its own.

Sometimes we are like this wayward sheep. We think we know best what to do and where to go. We choose to follow our own habits, even if they are wrong and selfish.

Many times in our waywardness we lose sight of our Good Shepherd. Jesus Christ seems to be far away. Even when we call to Him, He does not seem to hear. Yet, really, He is very concerned when we stray away and do not follow Him closely.

The best place to be is close to Him.

The Pet Lamb

A shepherd loves to play with his pet lambs. They are very dear to him. He holds them, hugs them, and enjoys having them close to him. Here you see the shepherd fondling his favorite little lamb.

You will be surprised to know that a pet lamb becomes almost like a shepherd's shadow. It follows him wherever he goes. It loves to be right beside him, just like a faithful dog. It knows his voice so well it comes when called, running and kicking up its heels with pleasure.

The shepherd sometimes carries special treats in his big pockets for his favorite pets. It may be a handful of tasty grain or some sweet clover he has plucked along the path.

It can be the same with us and God. He can be our best friend. We can become very, very fond of Him. Jesus Christ called us His friends. He just loves to have us come close and share our time with Him.

How do we do this?

He often calls to us by His gentle Spirit. He speaks to our inner hearts. He says, "This is the way I want you to behave." We can respond and obey. We can do what He asks. We can say to Him in reply, "Dear Lord, whatever you want me to do, I will do it."

This is to become a close friend of His.

You can enjoy following the Good Shepherd. He leads you along safe paths.

Yea, though I walk through the valley of the shadow of
death, I will fear no evil: for thou art with me;
thy rod and thy staff they comfort me.

Into High Country

Many sheep owners have what they call "summer range."
These are pastures far from the home ranch. Often the summer range is up in high hills. It may be miles away in the mountains.

Most of the year this country is cold and chilly. But for a few bright summer months it is lush, green with fresh grass and beautiful wild flowers. The scenery is wonderful. There are high peaks, silver streams, and shining snowfields.

A good shepherd enjoys having his flock thrive in this high country. But it often takes days and days to lead them through the long valleys to the high country. There are dangers along the way. I will tell you all about these as we go on. It really is not an easy trail, especially for lambs.

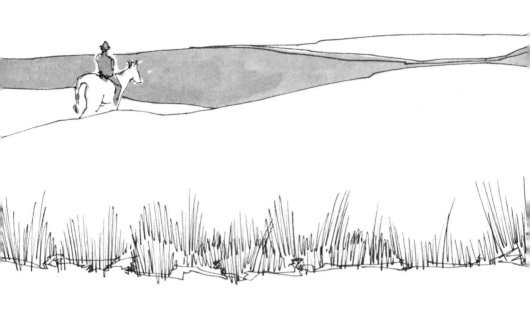

When our Lord Jesus Christ was living among us as a man, He said it would not always be easy to follow Him. He made it clear that *"in this world you will have trouble, but be of good cheer: I have overcome the world"* (John 16:33).

If you really want to follow Him, if you want to live a noble, lofty life, better and finer than you are now, it will cost some struggle.

You climb mountains with effort. You get into high country taking risks. You can become a "high level" person, following Jesus. There are exciting trails to tramp. Anything worthwhile costs effort. Try it.

Mountain Valleys

Every mountain or hill has valleys cut into its slopes. These valleys help to give each mountain its special shape. And strange as it may seem, very often the very best way to climb up onto the high country is along the valleys.

Have you ever noticed how highways follow the valleys to get over the ridges? The same is true of the trails where a shepherd takes his sheep. The valley paths are the easiest route, the best way.

The shepherd has been over this path before. He knows there are bound to be rampaging rivers sometimes. He knows there can be coyotes or cougars on the lookout for stray sheep.

But still it is the best way. It is his way. He is there to care for his flock. So all is well as they walk through the valleys.

That is how it is with us. God will sometimes take us through tough trails. He may ask us to face hard times. Perhaps we have to go into strange places or change schools or make new friends or lose some of our family. These all seem like dark, deep valleys.

Cheer up! You can face these bravely. You can walk through tough times and grow strong because Christ is walking beside you. You can become brave. You can live a noble life. Learn to go through hard, dark trials with the Good Shepherd as your companion.

The Long Climb

The trail to the top of the mountains is sometimes very long. It twists and turns around a hundred bends. It may take the sheep weeks and weeks to slowly climb from the low plains up to the high country.

All along the way the wise, skillful shepherd knows exactly where the safest paths are. He knows where to find the green, grassy glades among the trees where his flock can feed quietly, then lie down to rest. He knows where all the sparkling springs come bubbling out of the hot, rocky hillsides. He knows where every silver stream runs to refresh his thirsty sheep as they climb the steep slopes.

Because of his skill and care and guidance, all goes well. By the time his sheep reach the lovely summer range, they are sturdy and strong.

Our Good Shepherd, too, knows all about every trail in life He will take us over. He has been all over the ground again and again. He knows every dark valley or hard place you or I will ever go through.

In His great love and care for us He leads us through the safest way. He knows what is best. He knows where and when we need a little rest or refreshment. He knows how to encourage us to carry on, to keep climbing higher.

When the hard times are over we can look back and laugh. We can say, "See, look, how good God is! He is great!"

The Shepherd's Rod

On summer range in high country the shepherd is usually all alone with his sheep. They seldom see other people. As they move together over the wild meadows there are dangers different from those on the home ranch. There can be summer storms, blowing with gales of sleet and hail. There can be attacks from wild animals, or even snakes hiding in the grass.

To protect his flock the shepherd carries a club. It is generally called a "rod." It is a hard, heavy stick with a thick knob on one end. It is carved from wood exactly to fit his hand.

He becomes skilled in using this rod to drive away wild animals. He can hurl it with dead-eye accuracy. He can use it to kill a snake in a split second.

What do you think our Good Shepherd's rod could be? It

may surprise you. It is the powerful weapon of His own Word. All through the Scriptures, God promises us protection. His people can depend on Him.

Even when Jesus Christ lived among us He used God's Word to overcome enemies. Remember how He defeated Satan in the desert?

The same can be true for you. When you are in danger or under attack, learn to trust God's Word. Rely on Christ's powerful promises to protect you.

If you even memorize a scripture passage like Psalm 23, it can become a wonderful weapon. God will use it as His "rod" to defend you in difficulty.

The Shepherd's Touch

The "high country" days are special for the sheep. This is the time of year when the master gives each one extra attention. He watches carefully to see they are really fit and flourishing. He has time to check them one by one.

Because sheep have thick wool fleeces, it is not easy to tell from a distance if they are well. The good shepherd takes each sheep and opens its wool with his rod or his hand. He makes sure it has no wounds or disease. We call this, "passing under the rod."

As his rod opens the fleece, he gets right down to the skin. He can tell at once by his skillful touch whether the sheep is fit or not.

Strange to say, the sheep love this attention. They enjoy their owner's touch. They know it is for their good.

God has various ways of touching us too, just like sheep. Sometimes it is through His Word spoken to us by our parents, friends, or teachers. That word can open us up. It does away with our "cover-up."

The Word of Christ can touch us deeply. He has a way of getting below all our front and flimflam. He knows what we are really like.

At first some people are uneasy about this. As we get to know our Good Shepherd better, we learn that He always touches us for our own good. He does not draw near to hurt us, but to help us.

The Shepherd's Staff

A shepherd's staff is a long, slender stick with a crook on the end. It is one thing he always carries with him when he is in the high country. He uses it to help handle his flock.

Remember that out in the hills there is time for the shepherd to be very intimate or close and loving with his sheep. He uses the staff to draw any one of his flock close to himself. That way he can fondle and pet and examine it.

Other times he simply reaches out gently with the staff to touch and guide his favorite ones. It is a gentle gesture he uses to show the sheep he is near, that he is fond of them, that he is taking them into fresh pastures.

The sheep learn to love the touch of his staff. It helps to draw them all together.

God's staff is His own gracious, sweet Spirit.

Jesus told us that it is His Spirit who will be with us. He touches our spirits at the very center of our inner lives. It is His Spirit who guides us. He shows us clearly, using God's own Word, what we should do. He teaches us how to behave.

But perhaps best of all He helps us understand what God is like. He shows us how kind our Good Shepherd is. He can even use a little book like this to help draw you to Christ.

Never pull away from Him. Instead, draw close.

A Staff to the Rescue

In the high country there is not only beautiful scenery but also unusual dangers for sheep. Some of the sweetest grass and most tasty tidbits of feed are found on the tiny ledges of rock at the cliff edges.

Ewes and lambs that insist on pushing out into these perilous or dangerous places sometimes find they are in terrible trouble. They can't turn around. They can't back out. If they try to wriggle around, they sometimes slip and fall, crushing themselves on the cliffs below.

Other sheep push into thickets of brambles or fallen tree branches. Here their wool gets tangled, so they can't pull free.

Only the shepherd can rescue them by reaching out with his long staff. He tugs and pulls them back out of danger to safety.

We are a lot like that, aren't we? We decide we want something so badly we just keep pushing and pushing until we get it. We are determined to have our own way. At the time it may seem a treat. We don't pay attention to the risks we take. Then suddenly we are caught in a mess.

Let me tell you something. Don't be afraid to cry out to Jesus for help. He can rescue you. He will reach out to touch your trembling heart. He can set you free from fear.

When He draws you back to Himself, you will feel sorry for your waywardness. Don't do it again. Your stubbornness causes the Good Shepherd endless grief.

Thou preparest a table before me in the presence of mine enemies:
thou anointest my head with oil; my cup runneth over.

The High Tableland

Some of the finest sheep country in the world lies on high
"table" lands. This strange name is given to mountains that are
rather flat like a tabletop. In Africa there is a world-famous
mountain called Table Mountain.

A good shepherd will take time to go ahead of his flock to
make sure the mountain pastures are safe. One thing he always
does is to check for poisonous weeds. Some wild weeds are so
deadly that just a few mouthfuls will kill a lamb or ewe that
eats them. The "death cammas" is one of the worst.

If he has time, the shepherd will pull these out. Or he will
mark the places they grow and avoid taking his sheep there.
The reason is that lambs especially like to try almost every
new plant they see. Sometimes the ones they sample are poisonous and make them sick.

I want to share a special secret with you. If you remember it you will be spared trouble and heartache in life.

It is this. Our Good Shepherd knows every inch of ground in this old world. He knows exactly what temptations you may face. If you allow Him to lead you, He can keep you from bad habits that are dangerous. Obey His Word. Listen to His gentle Spirit. Do His will.

Please don't try every little tempting habit that comes your way. Your friends may do this. You don't need to copy them. Instead, do what is right.

Summer Storms

Summer in the alplands is a contented season for a flock. Most days are warm, sunny, cheerful. The mountain meadows are bright and green. The lambs enjoy the wild, new country. They grow rapidly. The ewes flourish and all the world seems at peace.

But the wise shepherd is still very alert.

He has been up here many times before.

He knows sudden fierce summer storms can blow up. Great dark clouds suddenly swirl around the peaks. Wind whistles through the valleys. It bends the trees, then chills the air. Quickly sheets of rain, sleet, and sometimes even hail will sweep across the hills. This terrifies the flock.

Very skillfully he will take his sheep into the shelter of some trees. There he will talk to them quietly until the storm is over.

It is that way with us. Some days start out cheerful and bright and happy, but suddenly change. Before we know what has happened, things seem suddenly to go wrong.

Perhaps your best friends unexpectedly start a fight with you. Maybe your teacher or Mother or Dad seems to be in a miserable mood. It is as if a storm of trouble blows up around you without warning.

Remember the Lord Christ can take you up in His arms. Turn to Him, saying softly: "Dear Jesus, I didn't expect this to happen. It's so sudden. Just enfold me in your arms. Keep me close to you until this storm blows over."

The Big-hearted Shepherd

If you paid careful attention to this story of the good shepherd and his sheep, you may have noticed one special thing about him. What is it?

It is how big-hearted and brave he is.

It takes a big-hearted person to be generous and kind.

It is the big-hearted shepherd who does not mind how much he suffers as long as his sheep flourish.

It is the big-hearted master who gives all his skill and strength and time to take care of his flock.

It is the big-hearted sheep owner who is all smiles when he sees his flock quiet and at rest.

This is what he lives for. This is what thrills his big heart.

Exactly the same is true of our loving Lord. He is our big-hearted, brave, and generous God. He gives and gives and gives His life, His strength, His love, His time, His attention to us.

He does this because He cares so deeply. Did you know He lays down His very life for you?

Not only did He do this once long ago on the cross at Calvary, but He is still doing it today.

Jesus is like the shepherd who quietly lives with his sheep day and night in the hills. He shares our lives everywhere. He is here. You can sense and know His presence. He makes Himself very real to anyone who turns to Him, talks to Him, trusts His company.

He smiles on you.

The Scourge of Scab

In some ways summer is the best time of the whole year for sheep. But in other ways it can be the worst time. This is the season when flies buzz around making life miserable for the sheep. Remember how I told you about that earlier in the book.

Summer is also the season for scab. Scab is a tiny, tiny bug that inflames the sheep's skin. There, sores grow and spread. They irritate the sheep. Those infected lose weight. They become sick. Worst of all, they can spread it to other sheep if they touch their heads together.

The only cure is for the owner to catch and separate each sick sheep. He applies an ointment or disinfectant. This makes a lot of hard work for him.

In the lives of people, sin is very much like scab in sheep. It often starts with something so small, so tiny, we hardly notice it.

Wrong ideas and wrong thoughts are harmful things we pick up from other people. Your playmates may put wrong thoughts in your mind. Maybe they think it is smart to cheat, lie, or laugh at people in trouble. Don't believe them.

The only cure for this is to keep away. Let the Lord Jesus give you His proper attitudes of kindness and concern. He will gladly give you His own kind Spirit. Just ask Him.

The Fighting Rams

Slowly but steadily the seasons change in the high country. Summer's warm, sunny weather turns cool. At night there is a silver touch of frost in the mountains. Gently the leaves on the trees and shrubs begin to flame color.

This is the season when the big rams become restless. They begin to shove and push each other around. They are eager to mate with the ewes so there will be strong, sturdy lambs early next spring.

As the rams fight for the favor of the ewes they crash and crack their heads together. Sometimes in fierce fights they actually kill each other.

The remedy the shepherd uses to prevent this is to spread grease or oil on their heads. When they try to fight, they glance off each other with little damage.

One of the reasons God says we are like sheep is because of the way we battle each other. Isn't it strange how we will

watch two rams fighting and exclaim, "Aren't they dumb animals?"

That must be exactly how our Lord feels when He sees us
proud, stubborn people fighting and quarreling. We are often
ready to hurl nasty remarks. We say cruel things to each
other. We may even start to use our feet and arms to kick and
punch one another in jealous anger.

There is really only one remedy for all this rage. Let Christ
put the gentle, gracious, healing oil of His own Spirit on your
heart. End the battling.

Autumn Glory

Autumn is such a wonderful season for sheep! The sharp frosts at night kill the bugs and flies. The sheep are no longer tormented by mosquitoes. Most days are clear and bright and brisk. The sheep do not have to seek shade from the burning sun. There is still plenty of lush feed because of gentle fall rains.

The countryside is beautiful. The early autumn storms leave a sugar coating of shining, fresh snow on the peaks. The trees turn gold, red, and bronze in their fall colors.

The whole world is beautiful, and glorious. Gently the shepherd begins to lead his flock out of the hills back down toward the home ranch. Most of the sheep are thriving, well and strong. And in the shepherd's own spirit there is a song of joyous pleasure.

This beautiful sense of peace and pleasure is what we sometimes call "having our cup run over," as if our lives are so full of love and joy and goodwill that they just spill over to touch others.

You know what it is like, don't you, when on certain days your whole life is so full of fun, laughter, peace, and good cheer you can hardly hold it in?

You just have to share your joy with others. You just feel so thankful to your Good Shepherd for all the beautiful experiences He gives you.

Just imagine how this makes His heart sing as well. It pleases Him so much to see you contented.

The Suffering Shepherd

Not every fall day is like Indian summer, with blue skies and balmy breezes. Some seasons, autumn storms come raging across the range with howling winds and stinging sleet.

The watchful shepherd keeps a careful lookout for these ferocious fall blizzards. They are called "killer storms." They come with freezing rain, followed by heavy snow. The sheep are chilled through, and sometimes trapped by dreadful deep drifts.

The good shepherd stays right with his flock through the fury of the gale. He leads them gently down out of the hills toward the home ranch. Often he breaks trail through the deep drifts himself.

If there is a weak or sickly sheep, he will give it wine or brandy from a flask. This warms it quickly. It encourages it to carry on through the stormy weather.

Several times I have told you that even though we belong to Jesus Christ, all of life will not be a picnic. There is no one in all the world who has just perfect, trouble-free days.

There will be storms for all of us. There are bound to be days when our skies grow dark. There will be times when we get "snowed under" with suffering or sadness.

We may feel so "down," so discouraged, so disappointed we want to give up. Don't! The Good Shepherd is right there with you in the storm. He will lead you, encourage you, warm you with His love. Be brave. Trust Him. Turn to Him for help.

Surely goodness and mercy shall follow me all the days of my life:
and I will dwell in the house of the Lord for ever.

The Shepherd's Goodness

Have you followed this story closely? You have seen how good the shepherd is to his sheep. When they were hungry, he gave them green grass. When they were thirsty, he led them to sweet waters. When frightened, he was there to protect them. When they were tormented by insects, he had a remedy to relieve them. If in danger from coyotes or cougars, he was there to save them. He always knew the best places to find the finest feed. He chose the safest trails into the high country. He was always aware of what his sheep needed.

All of their contentment was because of his care.

All of their good life was because of his skill and love.

All of their good life was because of his good life.

Let me share a special secret with you. It is exactly the same with us and our Good Shepherd!

Every good thing that comes to you in life comes from the goodness of God. The delicious food, the refreshing drinks, the shelter and love of your home and family are part of His care for you. The kindness of friends, the joy of play, the fun of life are His ideas for us. Every good gift, every pleasant surprise comes from Him. The strength of your young body, the keenness of your mind are His benefits to you.

Learn to remember this. Remind yourself always of your Lord's goodness. Thank Him every day. He will love it.

The Shepherd's Mercy

A good shepherd is also a kind and merciful person. He does not abuse his sheep. He is never cruel to them. He never neglects his flock.

This is because he is fond of them, and enjoys taking care of them. In fact, we say, "Sheep are his life." He actually lives for them.

The sheep in his kind care see something of his mercy and tenderness every day. The way he examines each one to be sure it is well and strong. The way he talks to them in low, gentle tones. The way he keeps them away from poisonous plants. The way he always picks them up and carries the weak lambs or sick sheep that stumble on the trail. In a hundred little acts of tenderness he shows his mercy and love for his flock.

It is all part of his very makeup and character.

He just can't be any other way.

Some people have very strange, twisted ideas about God. Somehow they feel sure He is terribly stern, severe, and even unkind. No, no, no!

When God came among us as the man Jesus Christ, everybody was amazed at His goodness, His mercy, His kindness. He healed the sick. He cheered the sad. He fed the hungry. He was a friend to sinners. He forgave those who truly wanted to change their ways.

Do you know something? He is still doing this today, His mercy is still coming to people everywhere . . . to you and me.

"Those of Golden Hooves"

Long ago, sheep were called "Those of Golden Hooves." This very lovely name had special meaning, because if a flock was well cared for by a good shepherd they would improve his land. Wherever the sheep went, the fields and pastures benefited.

Remember I told you earlier that sheep could do a lot of damage if left to themselves. They overgraze certain spots. They cut ruts in the fields. They pollute the places where they stay too long.

But with a good shepherd's care they can be very helpful. They eat up bad weeds. They spread their droppings over the barren hilltops. They keep pastures looking trimmed and neat like a park.

Wherever they go with their owner they leave the land behind them better than when they came. This really delights the shepherd. He loves to see his ranch in such beautiful shape.

It can be that way with us. When we are in Christ's care our lives can be a real benefit. We too can leave goodness and mercy behind us wherever we go.

People will be so glad we came along. Our little acts of kindness, thoughtfulness, and love can lift the spirits of others. The world can be a brighter, happier, more cheerful place because we passed through it.

Your Good Shepherd is so pleased when your footsteps leave behind the same goodness and mercy He has shown you. Pass on to your family and friends, even your enemies, the kindness He shows you.

The Faithful Shepherd

A good shepherd is also a faithful shepherd. He does not neglect his flock. He is always on the job. The most important thing in the world for him is to be with his sheep.

It does not matter whether it is summer or winter, he sees to it all their needs are supplied. Whether it is in the beautiful spring sunshine or in a howling fall blizzard, he is there to guide and care for his sheep. All year round, day and night, the faithful shepherd is with his flock to protect and provide for them.

He never fails them. He can be trusted. The sheep learn to really love him. They depend on him for everything. They are completely contented in his company. They enjoy just sharing his life. They have learned that the reason they have things so good is because of his faithfulness to them.

As we go on in our lives letting Jesus Christ guide us, we will discover the same things. He really is a good Good Shepherd. He is so true. He is so faithful to us. He does not let us down. He is always there to help. Even when things seem very tough or dark or sad, we find He is faithful to us.

He never disappoints us like our friends or family may do. As we go on walking with Him, following Him, we learn to love Him dearly. He becomes our best friend. We trust Him completely.

Coming Home

This story of the good shepherd and his sheep is almost over. We started out in early spring. Then the master put his special mark on the new lambs and sheep coming into his care.

You were told about the trouble he took to give them green pastures and fresh water. As summer came along, you traveled with them up into the high country. What an exciting adventure that was! In spite of raging rivers, wild animals, and fierce storms, the sheep were safe in his company. You heard about the glorious summer range, the flaming fall days. Then gently the flock came down again. All was well.

Now you see them happily coming back to the home ranch. Can't you hear them saying to each other: "This is such a wonderful owner! I'm going to just stay with him forever—I'll never leave his care!"

Those of us who are older than you feel exactly the same about God. We look back over the long, sometimes tangled trails of our lives. All the way our Good Shepherd has guided us. Our loving Lord laid Himself out for us wherever we went. We can see that it was He who kept us from danger. He made life exciting and wonderful. It has been filled with good times because of His goodness.

We feel absolutely "at home" with Him. We never want to leave Him. We want to be close, and faithful to Him forever. You can be the same.

His

As the seasons come and go, a great bond of love and affection grows between the shepherd and his sheep. As one year follows another, they become more and more fond of each other.

The kind, strong, good shepherd knows every one of them so well. They are his and his alone. They belong only to him. He gladly gives anything and everything he has for them. Why? Because they are his.

He just loves to be with them. They, in turn, enjoy being with him. Under his careful, watchful, skillful eyes they flourish. In his care, they are safe. They are content because he is always near.

They find peace and pleasure in his presence. Just to be in his sight sets all their fears at ease. To be his is to be secure.

This can be true for you too, my friends.

The last great secret I want to share with you about our Lord Jesus Christ is this: He is always here. He knows you as well as any shepherd knows his sheep. His gracious, gentle, kind Spirit wants to share your life.

You can come to the place in your heart where you know you really do belong to Him. You can talk with Him. You can listen to Him speak to you. You can see He cares for you. You can revel in His company. You can be HIS.

The Welcome

A shepherd is always adding new sheep to his flock. He chooses them with great care. He knows they become a part of his own life.

As the years go by, they will share all the exciting experiences this book has told you about. Can you remember most of them? Together the shepherd and sheep will travel the trails. They will revel in the beauty of the countryside. They will enjoy the seasons of spring, summer, fall, and winter.

For the sheep, it is just like being a part of the shepherd's family. There is no better place to be. It is just wonderful belonging to such a marvelous master.

It is exactly that way with our Good Shepherd. He stands ready, eager to welcome you into His family. Our gracious God longs to have you belong to His flock . . . His followers.

Perhaps while you were reading this simple story you felt a deep longing to belong to Him. Maybe you never really understood before how strong and kind and generous Jesus Christ really is. You may even have been a bit afraid. Now for the first time you really see what He is like. You see how God only wants the very best for you. He invites you to be His person.

Here is a very short prayer just for you: "Dear, loving Lord, I come to you now. Thank you for taking me into your family. I trust you to care for me all my days. Amen."

About the Author

Phillip Keller was born and raised in a remote part of Kenya, East Africa, where he developed a love for native tribes, wildlife, and exploration. Educated in British schools, he studied both science and agriculture at the University of Toronto, graduating with honors. After pursuing agricultural research and both land and ranch management in British Columbia, Keller was asked to make a study of the Masai land in East Africa. This resulted in his first published book on African conservation.

Following four more books on outdoor themes, Keller began writing Christian biographies and devotionals. He is the author of twenty-two books, including four best-sellers. Presently he devotes much of his time to writing, to photography, and to leading Bible studies for lay people. A citizen of Canada, he resides with his wife in British Columbia.